SPANGLED UNICORN

NOËL COWARD

An
anthology
by

NOËL COWARD

⋆

SPANGLED

UNICORN

⋆

*A selection from the
works of*

ALBRECHT DRAUSLER
SERGE LLIAVANOV
JANET URDLER
ELIHU DUNN
ADA JOHNSTON
JANE SOUTHERBY DANKS
TAO LANG PEE
E. A. I. MAUNDERS
CRISPIN PITHER
JUANA MANDRAGÁGITA
(*Translated by Lawton Drift*)

New York
HOWARD FRISCH
1982

PR
6005
.085
S6

ISBN o-910638-00-4

Library of Congress Catalog Card No. 82-083582

FIRST PRINTING

PREFACE

In selecting and arranging (and in some cases) translating this anthology I have been actuated solely by one dominant idea. That idea being, in a word " Progress ". Progress on and up as opposed to Along and Down. Progress towards a goal still beyond our actual vision but nevertheless luminous and radiant in those rare moments of inspiration which come to the aid of every real Artist be he either Poet, Painter or Musician. There is a War to be won and a Gulf to be bridged. The War lies between the creative Artists and the Philistines, the Gulf lies between To-day and To-morrow.

In this slim volume I have gathered together from all parts of the world fragments of thought, rich in beauty, the fruits of minds that are unafraid, clear and incisive in sophistication, strong in awareness of the age in which they live. Uncompromising in the integrity of their standards. Civilisation, for all those who have eyes to see, is passing through a period of Flux and Counter Flux. Values to-day as concrete as the Pyramids, to-morrow will prove to be ephemeral as smoke. Nations rock and tremble and rock again, fissures appear in the granite of accepted conventions and far away, down the wind, can be heard the voice of the people. Change and interchange and counterchange, something stirring far far below tradition consciousness, more positive and absolute than revolution as we know it—immeasurable in its portent insistent, challenging as the waves of the sea—relentless.

CONTENTS

LIST OF ILLUSTRATIONS

Janet Urdler

JANET URDLER

JANET URDLER

∾

INTRODUCTORY NOTE

JANET URDLER was born in Exeter on a very bleak day in November 1887. Her childhood was grim and church-ridden, nothing stirred in her consciousness of things other, until 1900 when she was taken to Dawlish in a bullock cart. It was apparently a sort of picnic. Later she was forced unwillingly to teach in school, and it was during these years of bondage that her "awareness" developed. Child psychology interested her, but obscurely, she seldom inflicted punishments on her pupils and she was remotely popular but in no way idolised.

When her mother and father died she left Exeter and wandered. There are few records of her journeyings; she was in

Lisbon in 1908 and Carthage the following
October. In 1912 she met Laura Todd (the
" Ariadne " of her early sonnets) and they
apparently went to Norway for a while.
When they returned War was sweeping
Europe. In an extract from a letter to Laura
in 1916 Janet says : " It is lovely here, very
peaceful and grey with rooks cawing, and
I suppose I am happy."

It was not until September 1920 that her
first book of Poems was published. Since
then she has written intermittently. *Lovers
of Brass*, in 1924, solidified her reputation,
which was further enhanced by *Bindweed* in
1927.

In an analysis of her work it is difficult
to avoid the obvious comparison with
Theodore Lange. There is the same twisted
earth consciousness and an almost identical
viewpoint on peasant maternity, but here I
venture to suggest the similarity ceases.
Whereas Lange (in everything but ' *The
Diver* ') was definitely retrogressive, Janet
Urdler goes forward and upward. The
three selected pieces in this book typify her

emancipation from the formal, in '*Hungry Land*', '*Hen bane, No Hen*' has been criticised as being reactionary, but to my mind, and I honestly believe this view is shared by most of her important contemporaries, this sudden spurt of almost sentimental irony is essential in illustrating the inverse ratio of the context. I have included '*Reversion to the Formal*' for no particular reason except that as an exhibition of verbal pyrotechnics it is immensely valuable, demonstrating as it does the importance of complete freedom of line. '*How does your Garden Grow?*' is too well known to require comment from me, or indeed anybody else.

JANET URDLER

❧

REVERSION TO THE FORMAL

EMMA housemaid sees the shepherdess shepherdess with crook lambs' tails up crying up trying gate hinges creak scream soul hinges scream creak no love no love Emma housemaid round red hands chimney smokes at sunset blue beads in thick sentimental air with children near women's children spherical butter skins and legs sausage swollen Job the Ploughman big Job big Job more children nuzzling and crying mother Emma mother Emma Emma no mother no love no love dairy-fed produce lush pasturage gate hinges scream creak happy scream love scream women scream Job goes home laughing Job big laughing Job windows shut door shut hot body hot air Emma housemaid no love waiting no love lonely.

JANET URDLER

❧

HOW DOES YOUR GARDEN GROW

SILLY lady with your trowel
Consecrating female energy
On small male plants
Outside your garden wall
Plains stretch limbless
To odd horizons
Inside there is peace
Sequestered foolish tranquillity
Shut away from vital urge
Stupid Arabis
Sanctimonious Hollyhocks
Bestial Lobelias
Concealing their obscenity in Prettiness
Like Vicar's daughters
In Organdie
What is there above but sky
What is there beneath but earth

Thick hot earth alive with jostling seedlings
And strange lewd bulbs
Silly lady with your trowel
How does your garden grow ?

JANET URDLER

❧

HUNGRY LAND

EARTH in chains and hunger
Tadpoles in Ponds
Cows retching
Drought
Famine
Milko
Oh No
Cattle come home
No home
Speed the Plough
No Plough
Hen bane
No Hen
Night shade
No shade
Only Night
Hungry Night

Elihu Dunn

ELIHU DUNN

ELIHU DUNN

࿊

INTRODUCTORY NOTE

ELIHU DUNN was born in Washington D.C. in 1896. He was educated there and then went West, then came back South. He was graduated from Deklopfer Burns High in 1920 New Orleans University A.B. 1924 Hoboken A.M. 1926, while in high school he attracted a good deal of attention, missed winning the inter-collegiate Poetry Contest prize by a hair's breadth 1923—1924—1925—1926—1927. Published *Blue Grass* 1928, *Blue Grass Revisited* 1929, *Blue Grass Again* 1930.

James Maddern Waller wrote of Elihu Dunn in 1929 " This man is a giant, the music of his words Crystallises in the air like bird song, he is the mouthpiece of his race calling them on to victory." Surely no greater

C

tribute could be paid to any constructive
poet. The selections from his work contained in this volume I think can truthfully
be said to represent more or less compre-
hensively Dunn's strangely powerful race
obsession. He is the champion of a cause
and will always be just that. To expect
him to write without bias would be as
absurd as to demand Meredith Flood to
compose chamber music. There is no com-
promise in these men.

ELIHU DUNN

୶

NECROMANCY

MA skin is black
As an ole black crow
Ole black crow
Vo dodeo do
Ma Pap was white
As de wind blown snow
Wind blown snow
Vo dodeo do
Ma Mammy was brown
As chicken soup
Chicken soup
Boop oop a doop
She knocked my Pappy
For a loop
For a loop
Boop oop a doop
Ma sis is pale

As a piece of Gruyère
Piece of Gruyère
Halleluia
But ma skin's black
As an ole black crow
Ole black crow
Vo dodeo do.

ELIHU DUNN
         TO ROBERT ANDREWS

HARLEM

YELLOW brown black
Limbs writhing in rhythm
Rhythm writhing limbs
Hot Momma Hey Hey
Where is Death if this is life
Night Life Night Death
Crazy 'bout you honey
Hey honey ma baby
African drums beatin' out soul rhythm
African blood coursing thru'
Dark streets
Hot dark breath
Shutters with light seepin' thru
Makin' black shadows
Black shadows of black loves
Saxophones moanin'

Groanin' groanin'
Where are de cotton fields
Where is dat blue grass
Where are dem ole oat cakes
No here Nigger
Hot Momma Hey Hey

ELIHU DUNN

❧

MA PEOPLE

Ma People
Call back ober yo shoulder
Way back to Jungle land
Come to Glory
Come with yo po hearts a-weary
Yo po souls a-stretchin' upwards to de light
Neber yo mind ma people
Neber yo mind when de white folks
Stand in the dusty streets a-nid noddin'
Der fool white heads
And a-laughin' and a-jeering'
De Lord lubs yo same as he lubs the King-
    fisher,
In de corn brakes
An de bees an de flowers in de Dixie fields
Ma people
Come on ma people

Lift up yo po hearts
Lift up yo po hands
Raise yo po eyes
The lord knows yo po backs is a-bendin'
Under yo po burden
An dat yo po feet is a-aching
In yo po shoes
Come on, yo po people
Ma People.

E. A. I. Maunders

E. A. I. MAUNDERS

E. A. I. MAUNDERS

෨෨

INTRODUCTORY NOTE

PREFACE TO LIFE

I AM me in one sense but not me in another sense because although sense is partially me it is not partially sense, but wholly sense, whereas I am not wholly me but partially me the sense of which is not sense entirely but too near truth to be not sense by which I mean that although not sense is far away from truth, truth is frequently not sense which makes me me more were it not that I was partially sense. Gertrude is Gertrude and I am me but we are the same in meaning, meaning being meaning to us and us being meaning to meaning and meaning meaning practically nothing to meaning people who are not people meaning Gertrude's bigness

is not my bigness any more than my littleness is Gertrude's littleness.   Gertrude's
littleness is little littleness as her bigness is
big bigness because it is impossible for
Gertrude to do anything by halves because
her one-ness is too complete to be able to
conceive of Twoness and she is big big in
her bigness and not really little little in her
littleness whereas I can change as smallness
changes not because I am really small but
because I know smallness whereas Gertrude
does not know smallness but only bigness
in living bigly as diametrically opposed to
living smally which may or may not mean
not living at all inside but only outside by
which I mean that Gertrude is meaning and
I am meaning but different and not the same
as opposed to being not the same and
different because differences in meaning are
negatives the same as rain and fish are
negative but not the absolute negative of
nothing which is more and not less negative
than Gertrude who is everything.

E. A. I. MAUNDERS

❧

MOSS

Sound is elliptical
Sorrow is sound
Sorrow is round
Curved like a ball
David and Saul
Knew about sorrow

Pain is a thing
Pieces of string
Tie them together
Wondering whether
Death is away

Thank you for nothing
Take it away
Over the hills

Back to beginning
Lying and sinning
Laughing and loving
Pushing and shoving.

E. A. I. MAUNDERS

༺༻

CURVE IN CURVE OUT

CATCH Time with a net
Nor yet embrace eternity
Like thin flute notes
Beads in ether—skipping down
Short stubby streets at evening
Without the vulnerable heel
Dr. Juno's Anvils
Babying Gods with comforters
And small edged clouds to ride
And jelly in sand the sea had left
Causing mirth in the basement kitchen
And making foolish extra editions
Trackless dust leaves no tracks
But animals know
And yet we do not know
Beyond small imagery
The history of the crooked stars
And wildly breaking light.

E. A. I. MAUNDERS
        TO F. TENNYSON JESSE

ൠ

CHURCH OF ENGLAND

GERTRUDE loves the Church of England
Font and Pew and Font
Hassock and Cassock and me
Pulpit pains are Gertrude
Gertrude is Ancient and Modern
And new and old.
Gertrude loves the Church of England
Choristers and boots and Adam's apples
Where through coloured saints sun dapples
Gertrude's cheek and hat bird
Gertrude's big umbrella
All the responses
Candles in sconces
Gertrude loves the Church of England.

Tao Lang Pee

CHANNING AND OLIVE WENCE. TRANSLATORS OF TAO LANG PEE

TAO LANG PEE

༄༅

INTRODUCTORY NOTE

Born Twang Ko[1]   B.C. 403
Moved to Pakhoi[2]   B.C. 398 or 399
Next heard of Tonkin[3] B.C. 360
And presumably died there.

1 NOTE.—Puriot seems sceptical and on page 2 announces definitely that Tao Lang Pee was not a man at all but the name of an obscure native sexual rite.

2 NOTE.—Professor Pung on the other hand in *The Bean Tree* and *Lotus Lotus*, Royal Geographical Society, Number 486 XLVIII, states absolutely definitely that Tao Lang Pee is still quoted in Thibet.

[1] See Dr. Ruben Field's *China*, page 218.
[2] See Maureen Dangerfield's *Up the Yangtse*.
[3] See Puriot's *Le Chine*.

TAO LANG PEE

" SAMPAN "

WAVES lap lap
Fish fins clap clap
Brown sails flap flap
Chop sticks tap tap
Up and down the long green river
Ohè ohè lanterns quiver
Willow branches brush the river
Ohè ohè lanterns quiver
Waves lap lap
Fish fins clap clap
Brown sails flap flap
Chop sticks tap tap

TAO LANG PEE

THE EMPEROR'S DAUGHTER

THERE she sits
Wao Ping
With her gold nails
Scratching memories
Lacquer memories of other days
Other lovers
Chow Ho of the casual limbs
Oo Sang Po of the almond teeth and sweet
 breath
Plong How of the short legs and careful
 eyes
There she sits
Wao Ping
In her scarlet Pavilion
Watching the gold carp mouths
Opening tremulously
Dying of love

Because it is Spring in the Lotus Pool
And Spring's lute is cracked
Cracked and broken with too many tunes
Love songs long since sung.

TAO LANG PEE

THE VOICE IN THE BAMBOO SHOOT

THE water is silver
Gliding softly by the Lotus pool
Softly softly softly softly softly
Little Princess Li Chung Ho
Daughter of a thousand stars
Imprisoned in an azure bowl
Where oh where is your lover
Your warrior lover
Lithe and tall helmeted for battle
Helmeted for honourable death
While you wait in your lacquer Pavilion
Tears dropping through the lattice
Tears like the jewels of Mei Tang Poo.

Serge Lliavanov

SERGE LLIAVANOV

SERGE LLIAVANOV

ॐ

INTRODUCTORY NOTE

IN writing of Serge Lliavanov it is hard to repress a shudder at the cruelty of a Fate which, when he was but four years old, struck him down and left him a hopeless cripple for the remainder of his brief and pain-ridden life. His mother, to whom he was devoted, died when he was five, and his father was exiled to Siberia two years later. Strange to think of the robust gaiety of *The Inn at Tobolsk*, *Kasha* and *The Cossacks' Ride*, emanating from that wasted diseased racked body. In 1915, just before he went blind he wrote *Freedom*, selected excerpts from which are included in this volume. He lived to see his dream of a Soviet administration realised and died peacefully in 1922.

SERGE LLIAVANOV

EVERY DAY

IVAN is lost in the snow
The wolves are howling.
Each bough bends beneath its weary load
Maria Ivanovitch rocks
Rocks by the fire and weeps
Ivan is lost in the snow
In the Nevsky Prospect the snow has been
    cleared away
To allow the Droshkys to pass
Over towards Oomsk the sky is red
Ivan went out with a basket
And swiftly became lost in the snow
In the squares of the city
And in the taverns
There is warmth by the stoves
And good wine
And the thick stocky women of the people

With strong square breasts
And jolly red cheeks
Red as the sky in Oomsk
And sturdy legs,
But Maria Ivanovitch rocks
Rocks by the fire endlessly
Ivan went out with a basket
And was immediately lost in the snow.

SERGE LLIAVANOV

❧

THEATRE PARTY

HERE we are. Programme quickly
Sit yourselves down
The Play begins
See the funny man
How he pretends to be hurt
No No Life is not so easy
Chocolate Panskys[1] for the asking
Delicious are they not
To while away the time
Before the funny man cometh again
To teach us to laugh at sorrow
Ha-ha-ha—ha-ha-ha—
Ho-ho-ho—ho-ho-ho.

[1] Pansky—small heavy doughnut.

SERGE LLIAVANOV

HARLOT'S SONG

Buy me. Buy me. Cheerio. Tip Top.
I will please you
With my happy laughter
And my gay Butterfly ways
Now bold now timid
How you will laugh to see me.
Run from you in mock fear
And then back again
Now sprite now woman
Which will you choose ?
Buy me.   Buy me.
Love is cheap to-day
Because fish must be bought at the market
Haddocks strong and fine
Small tender mussels for my mother
Buy me.   Buy me.
I am young am I not
Young and gay.   Cheerio.   Tip Top.

I will please you.
You cannot buy my heart
That belongs elsewhere
In the trees and mountains and streams
In the deep valleys
My heart is not for sale
It belongs to Michael Michaelovitch
And he is dead
And never again will I see him
Because he is so dead.
But my heart is with him
Under the thick warm earth
You cannot buy my heart
Bid what you will
But I will sing for you
See and dance for you
A dance of old days
One two three so
One two three so
There does that not please you
Buy me.   Buy me.
Cheerio.   Tip Top.

Juana Mandragágita

JUANA MANDRAGÁGITA

JUANA MANDRAGÁGITA

❧

INTRODUCTORY NOTE

It was Lawton Drift who just discovered Juana Mandragágita in Granada where she was living with two old ladies. The following year he brought her to Paris and installed her permanently in a small flat in the Rue des Saint Pères. In 1928 she went to Italy for a few days but was soon back again and working as diligently as ever.

I think it can safely be said that the years 1927 to 1929 comprised her Rhythmic Period. Later she forsook rhythm for the " Gothic," " Flamenco " (contained in this volume), belongs to this period together with " Que Verguenza " and " Cuidado Juanita ".

She is now at work on a book of Mallorcine legends which she hopes will be completed by the Spring of 1933.

JUANA MANDRAGÁGITA
              Translated by Lawton Drift.

☙

PICNIC NEAR TOLEDO

LIFE is a moment
A moment of life
Is Life giving
Life loving
Life is love
Love loving
Love giving
Cathedrals rotting
In hot sunlight
Mellowing for Death
Death giving
Death loving
Death loving Life
Life loving Death
Why are we waiting
Why sigh

Why cry
Why cry
Why sigh
Why sigh cries
Why cry sighs
Death Death Death.

JUANA MANDRAGÁGITA
Translated by Lawton Drift

∾

" FLAMENCO "

Ohè Ohè
La—a—aňňa
Lacalacalacalaca—aňň—aňňa
Nyah Nyah
Carista Carista Caristagarcon
Baňero
Paňero
Carista Carista Caristagarcon.

JUANA MANDRAGÁGITA
Translated by Lawton Drift

෨෧

TORERO

BULL Blood
Blood Bull
Red Red
Hola Hola
Gallant Parade
Ladies and Laces
Voluptuous faces
Music is played
Bull Blood
Blood Bull
Red Red
Hola Hola

Crispin Pither

CRISPIN PITHER

CRISPIN PITHER

ॐ

INTRODUCTORY NOTE

CRISPIN PITHER was born in Balacorry in 1892. His childhood was more or less normal, the childhood of a little Irish country boy chock-a-block with " fey " legends and superstitions, the traces of which are to be found to-day even in his most realistic and mature works. It was when he was twenty-two that he finally fell out with the Catholic Church. In 1915 he joined an Anti-Catholic organisation in Dublin which flourished but briefly. In 1917 he was at the head of the Anti-Catholic riots in Lausanne which might have had serious consequences for him had he not, by a strange dispensation of Providence, fallen suddenly ill and been forced to take to the mountains. There in almost ascetic seclusion he wrote his Trilogy

Sacrament which was never published.   In
1922 he organised an Anti-Catholic Club
in Seville which at the beginning gave great
promise of success, but later gradually lost
hold and was completely extinct by April
1923.   His early ballads were mostly written
between 1920 and 1924.

In 1925 he was back in Dublin organising
an Anti-Catholic mission for Manchuria, a
scheme which ultimately fell to the ground
owing to lack of support.

In 1927 he wrote *The Village Green* and
Peat.   The excerpts in this volume are from
the following :

" Pastoral."   *Early Ballads*.   Vol. 2
" Deidre."   *The Village Green*.
" The Whisht Paple."   *Peat*.

CRISPIN PITHER

෨෨

" DEIDRE "

DEIDRE the sorrowful smile of you
Deidre the Spring sweet guile of you
Calls me back when the red sun's failin'
Calls me back like a sea-bird wailin'.
Deidre the hard hard heart of you
Maybe the Banshee's part of you
From County Kerry to County Clare
I smell the smell of your tangled hair.

CRISPIN PITHER

֍

" THE WHISHT PAPLE "

As I were lolloping down the lane
On Michael Mulligan's Mary Jane
I spied a whisht man all in green
Bedad says I, 'tis a Ragaleen.
I lolloped on wid a troubled mind
Shure the Davil himself was close behind
Now Father Snuffy I chanced to see
" Mother of Jaysus," says I to he,
" The wee whisht paple are near at hand."
So he drew a circle in the sand
And squatted down in his cassock green
To make a mock o' the Ragaleen.
" Begorrah," says I, " 'tis all in vain
The Davil himself is home again,
So climb the Tower and ring the bell
For all of the souls you've prayed to hell."

Then Father Snuffy on bended knee
Strangled himself wid his Rosary
And there where a minute ago had been
A Holy Priest, was a Ragaleen !

CRISPIN PITHER

༄

" PASTORAL "

" AH, wheer are ye goin' Macushla Macree?"
Wid a toss o' her curls she's replyin'
" Och, I'm climbin' the mountain to Bally
   Macbog
Wheer me grandmother Bridget is dyin'
Wid a maringadoo aday
And a maringadoo ' adaddy o '."

" And whin you're returnin', Macushla
   Macree
Is it niver a present you're bringin' ? "
" Och, I'll bring ye a part of me grand-
   mother's heart
An' the part that I'm bringin' is singin'
Wid a maringadoo aday
And a maringadoo ' adaddy o '."

" And what if you stay there, Macushla
   Macree
An' lave me this soide of the water ? "
" Och, I'll lave you the pigs and jolly white
   legs
O' Father O'Flannigan's daughter."
Wid a maringadoo aday
And a maringadoo ' adaddy o '."

Albrecht Drausler

ALBRECHT DRAUSLER

ALBRECHT DRAUSLER

୨୧

INTRODUCTORY NOTE

ALBRECHT DRAUSLER was born in Breslau in 1914. In 1918 his family moved to Fribourg taking him with them. In 1919 he wrote his first poem " Die Armen " (The Poor). In 1920 came *Herren un Damen* and *Aufschnitt*, both works heavy with portent and strangely mature. School-days commenced in 1922, stormy school-days indeed. In 1924 he bicycled to Frankfurt and wrote *Liebes Kind.* The last two lines of which will always be remembered. " Thick hands that clawed my waiting heart, sex hands that pulled me over Death." Fetched back to school he was moody and impatient with his masters. In an extract from Professor Schneider's report in 1926 we read : " Drausler is brilliant in his studies but disappears for long periods, we are at a loss to know what to do with the boy."

In 1928 he wrote his first novel, 250,000 words in length, entitled *Tag*. This was subsequently publicly burnt in Strasbourg.

In 1929 he wrote *Brüderschaft*, three poems from which have been selected for this anthology. In 1930 he opened his veins and died in the school bathroom in Berne, fragments of his last poem "Leben und Tranen" on odd bits of paper littering the floor.

ALBRECHT DRAUSLER
(GEMÜTLICHKEIT)

FIRST LOVE

Lisa's eyes were full of trouble
When she looked at me last Sunday.
Girl's trouble
Her face was blotched and shiny
Where the tears had trickled.
She said she must go down to the Willows
Where we loved.
I do not understand girl's trouble
Perhaps I do not understand love
But hot bread I understand
And Apfelstrude and my mother's hot sweet
    belly
When she bends over in the abendstunde
And says " Curly head my Krochlein "
I asked her yesterday why Lisa had hanged
    herself

Down by the willows.
" Girl's trouble," she said, " Girl's trouble
Curly head my Krochlein."
Perhaps I do not understand girl's trouble.

ALBRECHT DRAUSLER

FREUNDSCHAFT

I WILL wear your cap
If you will wear my cap
I will give you raspberries
If you will give me raspberries.
I will caress your body
If you will caress my body
I will give you a sabre cut
If you will give me a sabre cut
I cannot give you my boots
Because Fritz loves them so
When I have a wife I will give her to you
And you will give me your heart
But not all of it.   Just a slice of it
Because of memories and Heinrich
And Spring snows on Eisenthal.

ALBRECHT DRAUSLER

"YOUTH"

FRANZI is fair and Gretchen is dark
And Marlchen's hair is like the Farmer's boy at home
But all heads are alike against the dark Osiers
Karl's head caught the flame of the dying sun
When I kissed his mouth
But it was redder when he came out of the Professor's room
The Frau Professorin was red too
When she pulled Gretchen to her
Why does Herr Dornpfner look at me like that
When he talks of München
In the Geography lesson
Yesterday there was hay on his waistcoat
Why does everything remind me of the Farmer's boy ?

Jane Southerby Danks

JANE SOUTHERBY DANKS

JANE SOUTHERBY DANKS

INTRODUCTORY NOTE

IN writing an introductory preface to Jane Southerby Danks it is odd to compare her early environment with that of her artistic contemporaries. Born in Melton Mowbray in 1897 she rode to hounds constantly, wet or fine, from the age of four onwards. Blauie's portrait " Musette on Roan " depicts her at the very beginning of her adolescence. From the first she shunned the company of the male sex, mixing only with her governesses. To one of whom Madeleine Duphotte she dedicated her first volume of Poems, *Goose Grass*. The Dedication is illuminating in its profound simplicity— " To you, Madeleine, from me."

Storm clouds in her relations with her mother began to gather on the horizon as

early as 1912, indeed in the May of this
year we find her in Florence with Hedda
Jennings then at the height of her career.
Her emancipation from home ties continued
and the breach had obviously broadened
in 1916 when we find her writing from a
whaler off Helsinforth to Mrs. Hinton
Turner (Libelulle) at Saint Cloud. " How
I envy you in your green quiet room. Here,
no lace no Sheffield plate, only tar and the
cry of gulls, but my heart is easier."

1924 finds her cosily ensconced in Bou-
logne where she first gained from the
fisher-folk the appellation " Knickerbocker
Lady."

In 1925 she published *Hands Down* to be
followed in the Spring of 1926 by *Frustration*.

In 1927 began her most prolific era in
Saint Tropey where in company with Zale
Bartlett and Thèrese Mauillac she wrote in
French her celebrated *Coucher de soleil pour
violon* and *Loup de mer*.

The poems included in this volume are
selected from her work of 1929–1930 just
after her quarrel with La Duchesse de la

Saucigny-Garonette (The " Madame Prac-
tique " of " Bon Jour ") and expressing in
their concrete outline her revulsion of
feeling against the Sous Realist School.

JANE SOUTHERBY DANKS

❧

LEGEND

SLAP the cat and count the spinach
Aunt Matilda's gone to Greenwich
Rolling in a barrel blue
Harnessed to a Kangaroo
Pock-marked Ulysses approaches
Driving scores of paper coaches
Eiderdowns and soda-water
What a shame that Mrs. Porter
Lost her ticket for the play
(Aunt Matilda's come to stay)
Prod the melons, punch the grapes
See that nobody escapes.
Tea is ready, ting-a-ling
Satan's bells are echoing
Father's like a laughing Ox
Mimsying a paradox

Aunt Matilda's pet canary
Freda, Sheila, Bob and Mary
All combine to chase the bed
Now that Aunt Matilda's dead.

JANE SOUTHERBY DANKS

SICILIAN STUDY

Dust
Lava
An old man
Two fish baskets
Tarentella Tarentella
Have you seen my blue umbrella?
Fanny left it on the beach
Out of reach, out of reach.
Careless Fanny, careless Fanny
Come to Granny, come to Granny.
Dust
Lava
Peppermint chimes
Dither through the valley
The Campanile totters
In yesterday's gentility.

JANE SOUTHERBY DANKS

RICHMOND BOATING SONG

APPLES and cheese
Come hold my hand
Trip it, Miss Jenkins, to Kew
The Wooden horse is panting—O !
But that's no argument
Look at Frank.
They brew good beer at the " Saucy Sheep "
With a derry dun derry and soon may be
One for all and all for one.
Parrots are blue in old Madrid
And barking tigers screech the song
Rum Tiddy, rum Tiddy
Peculiar.

JANE SOUTHERBY DANKS

OLD THINGS ARE FAR THE BEST

OLD things are far the best
So measure compound interest
On all infirm relations
And let them wait at stations
And never catch the train of Life
Through being too immersed
In conning passion's Bradshaws with " der-
   rieres " reversed
Toward the World of Strife.
So cherish Aunty Amy
And dear old Uncle Dick
And think of Mrs. Roger-Twyford-Mac-
   namara-Wick
Who bicycled to Southsea
When over eighty-two
And never left the handle bars
To contemplate the view.

Though Grandmamma may dribble
Don't point at her and laugh
She gave you Auntie Sybil
A train and a giraffe——
Old things are far the best.

Ada Johnston

ADA JOHNSTON

ADA JOHNSTON

INTRODUCTORY NOTE

NOTHING whatever is known about Ada Johnston.

ADA JOHNSTON

☙

THE NURSEMAID

I WISH to bathe my feet in the Turgid Stream
    of Life
And catch the cherry blossoms as they fall
One, two, one two.
The dreams that men have made
Live on in Tunnels underground
I think
A sword to the web of destiny
Would be a comfort in the winter months.
Parrot sound is angular
And wicked edges of the glass people
Crushed insensate
Have rattled like the tin of stones
Designs are futile
Why parody the inevitable
With mystic cherubim, afloat in treacle
By the Norfolk Broads.

ADA JOHNSTON

❧

SUNBURN

MABEL, Mabel,
How blue you are and yet how tawny brown
Your aspidistra feet are soft
And firm as oft
They pound my consciousness
To plastic emptyness.
But I shall borrow matches from the moon
When it is Easter Day.

ADA JOHNSTON

༂

TO RUDYARD KIPLING

TROLL cried the wind
Troll cried the sea
Troll cried the Emperor
What price me.
Thrilling to the touch of your wet, wet
    hands
(Abaft, belay, adjust the boom)
A little wind goes trickling through
The sunset unfurls like Madeira cake
Inviolable the Sanctuary
With a dish and a dash and the scuppers full
Throw the cook overboard,
He won't play.

ADA JOHNSTON

∞

DAWN

A THOUSAND Thanks my father said
Then flung his collar to the swine
That browse in Andalusia
It was raining that day
But beyond
The sun was carolling athwart the blue
And with a laugh we ran
And plucked the shimmering ropes of
  golden swings
It's wonderful the peace contentment brings
And all the ewes are white again
And stark with misty dew
And angular as sheets of light
Beneath the comet's cloudy vest
Innumerable buttons shine
Like pigs in amber.